Our recent popes have sought to reconnect the Church with the world, to be sure that it reflects and addresses the real concerns of people everywhere. Part of this effort has involved synods—gatherings of groups of bishops from around the world who discuss issues and discern ways to move forward.

Now, continuing this work, Pope Francis has called for a worldwide Synod where not just bishops have a voice, but all the faithful are asked to share their experience, strength, hope, frustrations, and questions so that the Church will be clearly hearing the voices of all its people.

Pope Francis is calling for the Church to grow as the body of Christ—filled with the Holy Spirit and focused on the needs of both the faithful and the world. We are all called to be part of it!

This booklet takes his words on the topic of synodality and offers a guide to help us all play our part in renewing the Church today. May these thirty reflections on Pope Francis's words open our eyes and hearts to this important mission.

The quotes from Pope Francis were chosen
by Deborah McCann, who also wrote the reflections
and the "Ponder" and "Pray" pieces.

TWENTY-THIRD PUBLICATIONS, a division of Bayard, Inc.;
One Montauk Avenue, New London, CT 06320.
860-437-3012 or 800-321-0411
www.twentythirdpublications.com.

Cover photo: M.MIGLIORATO/CPP/CIRIC

ISBN 978-1-62785-708-6 ■ Printed in the U.S.A.

 A Division of Bayard, Inc.

1 | JOURNEYING TOGETHER

*The Church is God's people journeying together
through the paths of history toward an
encounter with Christ the Lord.*

We have always been a pilgrim Church, restlessly searching for our home in Christ. At times, however, we have given in to the temptation to settle in, to become complacent and content with the way things are, and we have been satisfied with doing things the same way over and over. Pope Francis is calling the entire People of God to turn this around, to begin journeying anew as searchers walking together as equal children of God to meet and rejoice in the encounter with Christ.

PONDER

Am I too content and settled in my faith?
Have I stopped growing?

PRAY

God of newness and discovery, help us to find new ways to seek you, always mindful of the journey, not just the destination.

2 | UNITY, COMMUNION, FAMILY

*This is what we are called to: unity, communion,
the familial spirit that comes from realizing
that we are all embraced by God's love.*

In our lives as Catholics, we have become accustomed to responding to the top-down structures of the hierarchy—pope to bishops, bishops to priests, priests to people. The synodal practice Pope Francis is asking us to undertake works differently. He is asking us to come together as the children of God—all having something to learn from one another, and all having equal value in God's eyes, no matter where our traditional sense of position may place us. We are one body, one communion, one family.

PONDER

Whom do I see myself as superior to?
Or inferior to? What might this teach me?

PRAY

God of newness and discovery, open my eyes to your unconditional love, and help me recognize how much you love everyone.

3 | A PROCESS OF BECOMING

*The synodal process is a process of
becoming that involves the local Churches,
in different phases and from the bottom up,
in an effort that can forge a style of communion
and participation directed to mission.*

Pope Francis stresses that this practice of synodality is active, engaging, and exciting. It offers all of us, working together, an opportunity to become a new way of being Church in our world. We are called to open our eyes and ears and hearts to all the ways God is leading us so that we can all become more effective disciples. When clergy and laity all participate, everyone learns and grows. This deeper level of sharing may take some getting used to, but the fruits of the labor will be richly satisfying.

PONDER

Am I confident of my own voice as a person of faith?

PRAY

God of newness and discovery, help me to find and use my voice in your service.

4 | MORE THAN SIMPLY HEARING

*A synodal Church is a listening Church
that realizes that listening is more than simply
hearing. It is a mutual listening in which
everyone has something to learn.*

Pope Francis reminds us that the Holy Spirit is the force behind this entire process. The only way to hear the Spirit's voice is to listen for it, to put aside our own agendas and truly listen to what everyone has to share. This is a real chance for bishops to hear what their faithful feel and for the faithful to hear what issues their priests face. It is an opportunity for all involved to grow in the Spirit.

PONDER

Am I ready and willing to listen and set my preconceived ideas aside?

PRAY

God of newness and discovery, help me to grow beyond my complacency and to listen with an open heart.

5 | BE NOT AFRAID...

*When we are prepared to listen, we become free to
set aside our own partial or insufficient ideas....
In this way, we become truly open to
accept God's call to a new and different life.*

It is no accident that Pope Francis has called for
this worldwide Synod as the globe begins to come
to grips with a pandemic/postpandemic reality. At
this fragile time, we may be more ready to listen, to
recognize how the changes that Covid has brought
to our individual lives may open us to changing our
way of being Church, to discovering how to grow
together in new ways that reflect the Spirit of God.

PONDER

How has my life been changed by the pandemic?
Am I more open to accepting others?

PRAY

God of newness and discovery, help me to embrace
the changes I have made and to embrace the new
ones you offer.

6 | GUIDED BY THE SPIRIT

*The Holy Spirit guides us where
God wants us to be, not to where our own
notions would lead us.*

When he calls us to listen, Pope Francis is addressing every single person. Every person of faith has been gifted by the Holy Spirit with a task no one else can perform to build up the vibrant mosaic that is the Church. In all our meetings and gatherings, it is crucial that we be aware of everyone's contribution and that we invite everyone's participation. The Spirit speaks within us all and to us all. No voice is to be silenced.

PONDER

Have I ever been dismissive of others' ideas as unworthy? Have I let the Spirit speak through me, or have I stifled the impulse because I feel myself unworthy?

PRAY

God of newness and discovery, help me be open to the Spirit's guidance in everything I do.

7 | WHO'S IN CHARGE HERE?

Without the Spirit, no Synod.

Pope Francis makes it very clear that the listening we are called to do in the Synod process is listening to the Holy Spirit. "If the Spirit is not present," he says, "there will be no Synod." Our task is to get out of our own way and make ourselves open to what the Spirit is trying to do in and through us. We come to this process full of convictions and opinions. But are we so sure that our convictions are correct that we have pushed away the voice of the Spirit? The synodal process works only when we are all open to the Spirit, and the first step is really listening to one another.

PONDER

What notions do I have to set aside
to listen better?

PRAY

God of newness and discovery, help me and all the people of my parish listen to the voice of your Spirit.

8 | NO ONE ON THE SIDELINES

*All the baptized are called to take part
in the Church's life and mission. If the
People of God do not participate, any talk
about communion remains a fond wish.*

Pope Francis firmly believes that everyone who is
baptized has something to say about the Church
today, where it succeeds and where it fails, where it
does a good job of mission and where it lets people
down. In this Synod it is necessary that as many
voices as possible be heard, so that we all have a
clearer idea of how we can work together to foster a
vibrant, living Church for centuries to come.

PONDER

How do I really feel about the Church?
Does my parish reach out beyond the church
doors? Do I take part in its work?

PRAY

God of newness and discovery, help me get out of
my own way so that I can better see where you are
leading us as a people and as a Church.

9 | PARTICIPATION IS REQUIRED

We received this call to
participation in baptism.

One message that Pope Francis repeats whenever he talks about synodality is that everyone, by virtue of their baptism, is called to take part in the discussion of how the Church of the future will be shaped. It's easy to lose sight of our role and to leave decisions up to the "professionals." But the pope insists that in this process, the gift of our baptism has given us the right to be heard. Some may have more professional experience and training than others, but that doesn't lessen the power and impact of each individual voice. There are different gifts but the same Spirit, Paul reminds us. What better way to put our gifts to good use than united in communion?

PONDER

What gifts has God given me that I can share?

PRAY

God of newness and discovery, give me the courage to lift my voice so that, together, we may be the Church you call us to be.

10 | WE ARE EQUAL BEFORE GOD

*Everything starts with baptism,
which gives rise to the equal dignity
of the children of God.*

Baptism, Pope Francis reminds us, is the primary sacrament that marks us as God's own, and it is from this signing with water, oil, and the Spirit that we find our voice. Some among us have the opportunity to deepen their knowledge of the history and theology of the Church and are called to pastoral guidance. Some are called to consecrated religious life, but everyone is called to practice the faith wholeheartedly. Pope Francis stresses that all of us have some gift to share that will add insight to our discussions. Let us rejoice in our dignity as children of God.

PONDER

Have I ever really considered what a gift baptism is?

PRAY

God of newness and discovery, help me celebrate my baptism by putting myself at your service.

11 | OPEN OUR EYES, LORD

*A synodal Church calls for content, means,
and structures that encourage dialogue
and interaction within the People of God,
especially between priests and laity.*

These days, traditional models of clergy/laity
interaction are shifting. In fact, especially with big
changes in parish structures and fewer clergy to lead
them, our pastors and their staffs might welcome
suggestions on how to be more efficient and acces-
sible to those they serve. Pope Francis says the kind
of open dialogue called for by the Synod is essential
to building a more responsive Church. We cannot be
afraid to be vulnerable in our sharing. Such openness
can lead to great richness and deeper understanding.

PONDER

What do I know about how my parish works?

PRAY

God of newness and discovery,
help me do my part.

12 | PARTICIPATORY AND CO-RESPONSIBLE

A synodal Church is one that appreciates its own rich variety, gratefully accepting the contributions of the lay faithful.

"No one should be excluded or exclude themselves," says Pope Francis in his call for active, across-the-board participation in the synodal process. This is a challenge in many parishes and dioceses and for many of the faithful, but it can open the door to much fruitful growth. Think of all the people in your parish who teach children, consult on the finance council, proclaim the word, and share Eucharist. And think of those who, just by their presence at Mass, witness to their faith. We all have so much to share.

PONDER

Is there some way I can put my gifts to better use?

PRAY

God of newness and discovery, help me to notice how vibrant our parish already is.

13 | RISK #1: FORMALISM

The Synod is a process of authentic spiritual discernment that we undertake, not to project a good image of ourselves, but to cooperate more effectively with the work of God.

Pope Francis cautions that there are risks in the synodal process that we must avoid if our communication is to be effective. The first is *formalism*, which he describes as admiring the magnificent façade of a church without ever actually stepping inside. We have to set aside worries about how we might appear to others and take a courageous look into our own hearts. This process may reveal unpleasant and painful truths, but it is a necessary part of growing as the body of Christ.

PONDER

Have I been satisfied with a surface living of my faith?

PRAY

God of newness and discovery, help me to dig deep and to be unafraid of what I may find.

14 | RISK #2: INTELLECTUALISM

*The Synod must not be just the usual
people saying the usual things,
without great depth or spiritual insight.*

Pope Francis warns against turning the Synod into
an exercise of *intellectualism*, a "study group," where
it would be easy to rely on just a few to offer abstract
intellectual approaches to the deeply spiritual problems we face as a Church. This, he says, would mute
a great number of voices, "ending up along familiar
and unfruitful ideological and partisan divides" and
leading us to find ourselves far removed from the real
life experiences of the People of God.

PONDER

When have I settled for an "easy" answer
to a problem in my faith?

PRAY

God of newness and discovery, help me to be
courageous in my own faith experience so that
I might share it effectively with others.

15 | RISK #3: COMPLACENCY

*The danger of complacency is that
it leads us to apply old solutions
to new problems.*

Pope Francis doesn't mince words here: *complacency*—we've always done it this way—is "poison" for the life of the Church. The world is vastly different from what it used to be. As the People of God, we have been faced with issues that have made many of us question our faith—from the scandal of abuse to the role of women to figuring out how to worship together again after a pandemic forces us into isolation. To settle for "how we've always done it" runs the grave risk of not allowing ourselves to grow as a Church. Let us not be afraid to find new solutions to new problems.

PONDER

What lately has caused me to question my faith? How have I responded?

PRAY

God of newness and discovery, help me not to settle for old ways but to embrace the new.

16 | GOD'S WAY IS THE BEST

Consider God's own "style"—
closeness, compassion, and tender love.

After pointing out the risks of the abstract approach,
the intellectual approach, and the tried-and-true
approach to the synodal process, Pope Francis
reminds us that God's way is the best, and God's way
is simply the way of love. When we approach one
another from the viewpoint of compassionate and
merciful love, we can begin to learn to lower barri-
ers and begin real and fruitful dialogue. This will be
hard for many of us at the start, but a decision to be
less guarded and more open will make a huge difference in the Synod's ultimate success.

PONDER

When have I observed God's unconditional love
in action?

PRAY

God of newness and discovery, help me to be
open in my communicating, so that you can speak
through me.

17 | OUR HALLMARK: SERVICE TO OTHERS

*The only authority for the disciples of Jesus
is the authority of service, and the only power
is the power of the cross.*

We must never forget, Pope Francis reminds us, that we are all disciples, called by our baptism to serve others. When we begin to see this dialogue of the Synod leading to unity and communion, we naturally progress to mission. Starting with our interactions with one another, ensuring that the wider parish is represented and contributing to the diocesan discussion, and relying throughout on the guidance of the Spirit, this synodal process will help us deepen our lives into a new way of being Church.

PONDER

Am I able to look at the wider picture of where this process may lead us as a parish?

PRAY

God of newness and discovery, fill me with hope that our work is worthwhile.

18 | A CHURCH WITH OPEN DOORS

It is important to keep an open mind toward all those who have the desire and willingness to be encountered by God's revealed truth.

In 2019, Pope Francis spoke about a synodal process while addressing the issue of effective youth ministry. He said then that it was not necessary to adopt all the beliefs and teachings of the Church to be part of the discussion. What mattered was one's willingness to entertain God's message. He realized that many young people have problems and issues that the Church was not addressing—and the way for the Church to address them was to listen with open minds and hearts. That is his call today to all of us as we seek to grow together.

PONDER

Do I attract others to the faith by my actions?

PRAY

God of newness and discovery, help me to listen well so that I can make a difference.

19 | LIVING OUR VOCATION

*To live our vocation, we need to foster
and develop all that we are.*

Pope Francis stresses that developing all that we are
does not mean that we have to invent ourselves from
scratch. God has already given us our true selves. Our
task is to look inward to find that self in God's light
and live that reality. When we discover and nurture
the person God has created us to be, we can begin to
see where and how we fit into God's plan. And when
we put our gifts courageously and confidently at the
service of the Church, we can begin to make a real
difference, not just in the Church of tomorrow, but
in the Church of today.

PONDER

Have I ever tried to see myself as God sees me?
What's holding me back?

PRAY

God of newness and discovery, give me the courage
to be confident in sharing my gifts so that all I do
may give you praise.

20 | SHARING THE LIGHT

*Your vocation enables you to bring out the best
in yourself for God's glory and the good of others.*

We all have a vocation, Pope Francis reminds us.
Relatively few of us will be called to priesthood or
consecrated life. But all of us are called to live up to
our baptismal promises and to find whatever is best
in ourselves to put at God's service. In the synodal
process, Pope Francis hopes we will all discover how
we can help one another grow into a Church that
is responsive to all the faithful and a beacon in our
world. One, holy, catholic, and apostolic—we have
a long way to go to fully realize this, but by listening
and working together, we will find the tools we need.

PONDER

Do I truly understand the purpose of this Synod?
Am I ready to meet and greet others as brothers
and sisters?

PRAY

God of newness and discovery, help me to do my
part to reveal God's glory in all that I do.

21 | FINDING OUR WAY

Simply doing things is not the point.
Doing things with meaning and direction is.

Pope Francis isn't calling for this synodal process just so we can all feel like we're involved in the Church—as important as that is. No, he is hoping for clearer "meaning and direction" for our future together. In the same way, it is important to study what has worked as well as what hasn't. Where have people been listened to, and where haven't they? Which plans in our own parish have grown out of greater sharing and which have seemed imposed, and why? Rushing to put plans into action isn't the point. The point is to make sure that whatever we decide to do is firmly rooted in the guidance of the Spirit.

PONDER

How might the synodal process help me find meaning and direction in my own life too?

PRAY

God of newness and discovery, help me be part of this worldwide effort to listen to your Spirit.

22 | GAINING PERSPECTIVE

When we journey together, young and old,
we can be firmly rooted in the here-and-now,
revisit the past, and look ahead.

One advantage to listening to those who have spent their lives studying the Church is that we can learn from history. Pope Francis says that revisiting the past allows us to examine and heal old wounds caused by problems that still affect the Church. It also helps us look to the future with new eyes, to work toward that future with an enthusiasm that will "cause dreams to emerge, awaken prophecies and enable hope to blossom." The voices of experience can help us all discern the way forward.

PONDER

Have I spent much time studying the history of the faith? What lessons has it taught me?

PRAY

God of newness and discovery, help me learn and appreciate how you work in history.

23 | RECEIVING AND LIVING THE GIFT OF UNITY

As the one People of God, let us journey together, to experience a Church that receives and lives this gift of unity and is open to the Spirit's voice.

"[A] Church that receives and lives this gift of unity...." These are powerful words from Pope Francis about what he hopes the Synod will bring about. But this unity is dependent on being open to the Spirit's guidance. Pope Francis hopes that our progress of journeying together on the local level will lead to participating in the Church on the global level—where the gifts of every nation will only deepen our unity.

PONDER

How much do I know about the Church in other countries? Or in other regions of my own?

PRAY

God of newness and discovery, help me to find something new in every day.

24 | THE FRUITS OF OUR LABOR

*If we journey together, we can learn from
one another, warm hearts, inspire minds
with the light of the gospel, and lend
new strength to our hands.*

Unity, communion, mission—these are the hallmarks of the synodal process, and Pope Francis is confident that a true effort on the part of the whole People of God can make this a reality for our Church. We have all known people and places that inspire us by the warmth and generosity of spirit they express. Their enthusiasm is catching—we want what they have. Pope Francis reminds us that by opening our hearts and minds to one another and to the Spirit, we can help the Church survive and thrive in the years to come. Let us not be afraid to grow.

PONDER

How can I best do my part to help the Church grow?

PRAY

God of newness and discovery, let your Spirit fill me with hope and purpose.

25 | OPPORTUNITY #1:
A SYNODAL CHURCH

*Let us experience this moment of encounter,
listening, and reflection as a season of grace.*

Pope Francis spells out three opportunities that can
be ours when we embrace the idea of synodality for
the Church. The first is just that: *becoming a synodal Church*, a place where everyone feels wanted,
welcomed, and at home. The Church will become
a place where all participate, not only a chosen few.
This applies to all time, not just to this occasion. He
foresees a Church where all work together, a season
of grace where our openness to one another allows us
to hear and respond to the Spirit's prompting.

PONDER

Am I ready to take this process of synodality to
the next level? Am I ready to live this way of being
Church?

PRAY

God of newness and discovery, help me to remain
open to all the ways you are guiding me.

26 | OPPORTUNITY #2:
A LISTENING CHURCH

*A listening Church gives us the freedom to stop
and listen, removed from our regular routine.*

One of Pope Francis's favorite words is "listen."
In naming *being a listening Church* as the second
opportunity to grow out of the Synod, he is making
it clear that whatever openness we reach throughout
the synodal process is only the beginning. From here
on in, being willing and ready to hear others in all
circumstances is to be our trademark. Remaining
open to listening can lead to fruitful discernment
over all parish decisions. When we achieve this, we
will fulfill our call to share the Good News of the
gospel because people will see us living it.

PONDER

In what areas of my life do I need to improve my
listening skills?

PRAY

God of newness and discovery, help me to learn by
listening and only then to respond.

27 | OPPORTUNITY #3: A CHURCH OF CLOSENESS

The Lord's Church is a Church of closeness, with attitudes of compassion and tender love.

When we engage in true listening, we will become, as Pope Francis says, *a Church of closeness.* In addressing the opening of the Synod, he goes on to state what this Church will look like. A Church of closeness will build ties of friendship locally and globally. It will deal with problems and needs that exist today, not observing from the sidelines, but diving into their midst. It will reach out to mend broken hearts compassionately and with love. This is the Church Christ calls us to be.

PONDER

Whom do I pull back from in my daily interactions? How can I be more responsive?

PRAY

God of newness and discovery, help me remember your love for me so that I may better love others.

28 | MANY VOICES, ONE SONG

*Always remain attentive to
God's melody in your life.*

In thanking a choir that had sung for him on the occasion of meeting with an ecumenical delegation to Rome, Pope Francis said how delightful it was to listen to their music. He used this as an opportunity to mention the "learning to listen" that he hoped would come out of the Synod. And he asked that we all "listen to the melody that the Lord has composed in your life." Perhaps without realizing it, he said, listening with open hearts would lead to touching the mystery of God, the mystery of "love, the love that in Jesus Christ finds its splendid, full, and unique sound."

PONDER

How can I listen better to God singing within me?

PRAY

God of newness and discovery, help me to find the song that is only mine to sing, so that I may lift my voice and heart in harmony with all.

29 | PRACTICE MAKES PERFECT

*The Church needs your momentum,
your intuitions, your faith.*

Pope Francis urges us to listen for the Spirit's guidance as we enter this exciting and challenging moment for the Church. It is up to each of us, as the People of God, to listen well so that our decisions will be made for the good of the entire Church. The Spirit is leading us on untried paths—it takes courage to begin and more courage to persevere. But the pope is confident that if we give ourselves over to this new way of being Church, we will have achieved something great. "And when you arrive where we have not yet reached," he says, "have the patience to wait for us."

PONDER

What will this new Church look like?
Am I ready to be part of it?

PRAY

God of newness and discovery, open my heart to the wonders you have in store.

30 | WORDS OF LIFE ON OUR LIPS

*Let us not lose our enthusiasm, water down the
power of prophecy, or be satisfied with useless
and unproductive discussions.*

In a stirring prayer about his hopes for the Synod,
Pope Francis asks that the Church not be "beautiful but mute" but rather rejoice in what we discover
about one another and let that inspire us. He hopes
that we consider all voices as sharing prophetic
truths and that we fill all discussions with the Spirit's
power. We stand on the threshold of a Church filled
with the promise that comes from the presence of
all the People of God, united in communion and
mission. Let us respond with joy!

PONDER

What will this process bring to our parish
and our world?

PRAY

God of newness and discovery, help me do my part
to bring about a Church that reflects your love!